T0131668

HE IS BACK

TEN PIECES OF EVIDENCE

SALTY YEOM

ARCHWAY
PUBLISHING

Archway Publishing books may be ordered through booksellers or by contacting:

Archway Publishing
1663 Liberty Drive
Bloomington, IN 47403
www.archwaypublishing.com
844-669-3957

All Scripture quotations are taken from the King James Version.

ISBN: 978-1-6657-2898-0 (sc)
ISBN: 978-1-6657-2899-7 (e)

Library of Congress Control Number: 2022915951

Print information available on the last page.

Archway Publishing rev. date: 9/30/2022

CONTENTS

Prologue... vii

ACT 1

First Evidence:
War 1

Second Evidence:
Famine 3

Third Evidence:
Pestilence and Plague 8

Fourth Evidence:
Earthquakes 12

Fifth Evidence:
Iniquities 14

ACT 2

Sixth Evidence:
False Christs.. 28

Seventh Evidence:
Cross Again... 47

Eighth Evidence:

Resurrection Again 49

ACT 3

Ninth Evidence:

New Jerusalem 53

Tenth Evidence:

New Name of Jesus 54

Epilogue... 57

PROLOGUE

"'Tell us, when shall these things be? and what shall be the sign of thy coming, and of the end of the world?'

"And Jesus answered and said unto them, 'For nation shall rise against nation, and <u>kingdom</u> against <u>kingdom</u>:

and there shall be famines,
and pestilences,
and earthquakes, in divers places.
And because iniquity shall abound, the <u>love</u> of many shall wax cold.'" (Matthew 24:3–15 KJV)

The signs of Jesus coming are below:

1. Wars
2. Famines
3. Pestilences (plague)
4. Earthquakes
5. Iniquities

Now the signs are being fulfilled
I was born in South Korea in 1976. When I was growing up,

especially in South Korea, competition for university entrance exams was fierce and competition for employment was fierce. I got sick during this time. I was exhausted from running only to win the competition. I read the Bible for the first time around 2008, when I was recovering from the disease.

I majored in science in college and studied a lot to get a job, but I couldn't find my way. But through the Bible and Jesus, I discovered the essential way of life. After that, I met a teacher and learned the Bible deeply, left him, and in the spring of 2020 I got a message from Jesus.

In addition to the evidence already mentioned, I will present conclusive and additional evidence for the fact that Jesus has returned.

ACT 1

FIRST EVIDENCE:

War

In that day there will be *wars*, famines, earthquakes, and plagues. (Matthew 24:7, KJV; Luke 21:11, italics added)

Russian invasion of Ukraine in 2022:
Number of deaths: at least 46,000
Beach meditation number of people: 1.2 million
Number of missing persons: at least 400
Number of refugees: at least 12 million
Number of building collapses: at least eighteen hundred
Property damage in dollars: 564.9 billion
(April 4, 2022)

Prior to the twentieth century, transportation was not developed. So the scale of the war was not large. However, from the twentieth century onwards, transportation developed, and the scale of the war grew. And great wars were often fought.

World War I: 1914–1918
World War II: 1938–1945
Korean War: 1950–1953

Vietnam War: 1955–1975
Gulf War: 1990–1991
9/11 incident: 2001
2006 Israel-Lebanon War: 2006
Fatah-Hamas conflict: 2006–present
War in Somalia: 2006–present
Second Tuareg Uprising: 2007–present
2007 Ogadan Conflict: 2007–2009
Conflict in Lebanon: 2007
Gaza War: 2008–2009
2008 South Ossetian War: 2008
Libyan Civil War: 2011
Libyan Civil War: 2014–present
Syrian Civil War: 2011–present
Donbass War: 2014–present
Yemen Civil War: 2015–present
Nagorno-Karabakh War: 2020
Ukrainian-Russian War: 2022

SECOND EVIDENCE:

Famine

In that day there will be wars, *famines*, earthquakes, and plagues. (Matthew 24:7; Luke 21:11, italics added)

In 1929, after World War I, the Great Depression came.
In 1950, there was a Korean famine after the Korean War.
In 2008, the US financial crisis was caused by trade war.
In 2022, there was famine due to the Russian-Ukrainian war.
When there is a war, there is always a famine.
The following are related materials.

The world economy was stagnant due to World War I, but it revived from the early twenties and prospered throughout the twenties. This is especially true of the US economy. The United States enjoyed an unprecedented boom from 1923 to 1929. In the meantime, industrial production doubled, and GDP increased by 40 percent. This is because the United States made a lot of money selling munitions and food to European countries while there was no damage from the war.

However, this is not the case in all countries or sectors. In particular, the agricultural sector was facing a crisis through the twenties. This is because the arable land has greatly increased, thanks to the increased demand from the exhibition. So between 1924and 1929, international wheat prices fell by almost half. The same was true of the mineral products market, where a lot of investments in mines were made due to wartime demand.

Also, the boom in the world economy, including Europe, in the late 1920s was not so healthy. This is because it relied mainly on the export of US capital and US imports.

In particular, Europe was heavily dependent on the US economy. This is because American capital flowed into Germany from 1924 and greatly restored the German economy, which in turn led to the economic growth of the whole of Europe.

The booming US economy also expanded the stock market. Stock prices rose steadily for five years from 1924 and continued to rise in 1928. But it didn't last long.

This is because the stock market, which was experiencing a speculative boom, suddenly collapsed on October 24, 1929. On this day, which was called Black Thursday, the stock bubble that soared to the ceiling burst, signaling the end of the boom.

This was a devastating blow to American stock investors, and the impact gradually spread to the rest of the economy. In addition, because America occupies a large proportion in the global economy, it developed into a global economic recession. The Great Depression had begun.

So what was the cause of the economic crisis? One factor was that America's wealth distribution in the twenties was extremely unequal.

In 1929, the wealthiest 1 percent of the population owned 60 percent of the national wealth, which is about double compared to what it was in 1963 (32.5 percent) and in 1983 (41.8 percent).

The savings of the top sixty thousand households was higher than the savings of the bottom 25 million households. A larger share of national income was thus concentrated in the upper classes, and the economy became increasingly dependent on their consumption.

Still, their consumption was not large enough to revitalize the economy. As the economy boomed and corporate profits grew quickly, entrepreneurs greatly expanded their facilities. As a result, companies were producing more than consumers could buy.

In particular, overinvestments were made in the automobile, steel, and construction sectors. However, in 1928 and 1929, as consumption did not keep up with production, inventories increased. As a result, production fell, and employment declined.

Under these circumstances, workers, farmers, and the middle class did not have the economic strength to sustain the high economic growth of 1928–29. They could not increase consumption.

The income of lower classes accounted for 16 percent of the total national income in 1919 but decreased to 9 percent in 1929. The wages of workers rose by about 10 percent in the twenties, but their share in total national income fell compared to the early twenties.

The introduction of new labor-saving machines created technological unemployment.

Unemployment was relatively high throughout the twenties, remaining at 7 percent. Continued unemployment meant poverty and reduced purchasing power, as there was still no unemployment insurance or federal welfare plans.

Another inherent weakness of the US economy was in the realm of international economic policy. During World War I, the United States was the world's major creditor, as European countries borrowed billions of dollars from American banks and treasuries.

However, the United States did not change its trade policy in the context of the 1920s. Throughout the 1920s, the United States built high tariff barriers against major European and Latin American countries and had a trade surplus.

This was to protect their own industries and agriculture. And the US lent more money to entrepreneurs and governments in other countries to take on debt and buy American products.

When the panic began, American capitalists who lost money not only refused to issue new loans or make loans to foreign countries but also refused to extend loans that had expired.

Foreign debtors, who could no longer get money, were forced to go bankrupt. As a result, US exports also plummeted.

The sharp decline in international trade and the collapse of the stock market were the main causes of the Great Depression.

After the Korean War, Korea was the poorest country. In the 1960s, the country's national income was far behind that of other developing countries in Asia, such as the Philippines and Malaysia, as well as other African countries.

According to World Bank statistics, sixty years ago, in 1962, Korea's per capita gross national income (GNI) was $110 (about 120,000 won), which is less than 1/200 of this year's (estimated about $23,000). Even now, the income level fell behind Africa's Ghana ($190) and Gabon ($350), which are among the poorest countries.

The first role model for the Korean economy was the Philippines. Although GNI per capita is now one-tenth that of Korea, the average income of the Philippines at that time was twice that of Korea, so it was the object of envy.

The Russia-Ukraine War in 2022

Even more serious are the signs of a prolonged war. In February, Russia invaded Ukraine, and although the two countries began negotiating an armistice, no conclusion has been reached by the time of this writing. This raises the possibility of missing the sowing time. In addition, 30 percent of arable land was damaged as battlefields, and there is also a shortage of farm workers because of the large number of people who became refugees. The impact on the global food market alone could drive an additional 7.6 million to 13.1 million people into hunger.

Around 2000, the era of unlimited competition between individuals was entered, although no guns were raised due to the spread of neoliberalism. This resulted in a wealth imbalance, and the population that suffers from famine (starvation) rose sharply.

Due to high prices, people suffer from hardship, unless they are extremely wealthy. And internal civil war continues. Conflicts between countries continue.

THIRD EVIDENCE:

Pestilence and Plague

In that day there will be wars, famines, *pestilences* and
earthquakes. (Matthew 24:7; Luke 21:11, italics added)

The Black Death occurred during the thirteenth and fourteenth
centuries, killing a third of Europe's population in the Middle Ages.

For the first two months, the lung plague was prevalent. The
patients vomited blood from a high fever and died within three days.
After that, the Black Death came.

With high fever, an egg-sized boil occurred in the armpit or
groin, pus flowed from there, and death occurred within five days
of the onset.

The death toll was so high that it was called "big death" in the
West. It was known that the Black Death was originally endemic to
southwestern China or central Asia. But how did the Black Death
come to Europe?

Scholars suggest three reasons for this.

The first is that when the Mongols invaded Europe, the plague
bacillus came along with them. When the Mongol Empire's Kipchak
army attacked the port city of Kappa on the Black Sea, the Black
Death spread when the bodies of soldiers who died from the Black

Death were thrown into the fortress. The Mongol Empire was engaged in a kind of germ warfare.

The second is that trade between Asia and Europe was prosperous at the time, and it was spread by merchants traveling between Asia and Europe via the Silk Road.

The third is that they moved by sea route, which was used for trade between Asia and Europe. Of these, the most fatal result was the transmission through sea routes.

In 1347, a ship from the Black Sea arrived on the island of Sicily in southern Italy. The ship was already full of dead bodies from the Black Death.

When the ship reached the port, the mice in the ship ran onto land and spread the plague everywhere. At that time, European cities were full of filth, they were infested with rats, and people did not wash well. Famine continued, and many people became malnourished.

It was an environment where contagious diseases could easily spread. If even one member of the family got the plague, the whole family would die at once.

Even those who attended the funerals of plague victims or took part in the burial of their bodies were not spared the plague. Countless lives were lost in Europe, especially Italy, Austria, and France.

The deaths were so great that the streets were flooded with corpses that could not be buried, and the plague spread even further.

The Black Death, which started in southern Europe in 1347, spread to northern Europe and Africa, and in 1353, it also polluted Moscow. Still, there was no way to cure the Black Death.

People originally thought the Black Death was a punishment from God. Then, they realized that the Black Death was transmitted through ships coming from abroad, and they quarantined foreign ships in the port.

Only those who survived in good health for forty days in a boat on the sea were allowed to enter the land.

Since the incubation period of the plague is ten days and death occurs within five days of onset, the forty-day quarantine period was very effective in preventing transmission.

It is in this historical background that the English word "quarantine" was derived from the Italian word *quarantenaria*, meaning "forty days."

December 1917–April 1919: Spanish Flu

The 1918 Spanish flu, the first pandemic of the twentieth century, continued until April 1919.

At that time, 500 million people, or 27 percent of the world's 1.9 billion people, were infected with this flu. Globally, the death toll is estimated to be between 40 and 50 million. The Spanish flu virus spread not only to continental Europe, but also to the South Pacific Islands and the Arctic via the United States, Japan, India, and China. The epidemic spread at the end of World War I.

The Spanish flu occurred at the end of 1917, spread throughout 1918, and ended in April 1919. In the course of the process, three diffusion waves were drawn. It spread in June-July 1918 and seemed to stop for a while.

From October of that year to the beginning of January of the following year, it spread into a pandemic. As the years changed, it spread again in early 1919, but disappeared like snow in April (source:wiki).

COVID-19

In March 2020, a pandemic was declared; there were continuous mutations, and there is no end in sight yet.

COVID-19 (as of April 30, 2022)

Confirmed cases: over 500 million

Deaths: 6 million or more

The World Health Organization (WHO) has warned that the number of confirmed cases of novel coronavirus infection (COVID-19) is just the tip of the iceberg and that we must remain vigilant.

WHO Director-General Tedros Adhanom Ghebreyesus said at a press conference, "The number of confirmed cases of COVID-19 is increasing in some countries, even though diagnostic tests have declined in some countries. It means that is only a fraction of it."

FOURTH EVIDENCE:

Earthquakes

"In that day there will be wars, famines, pestilences and earthquakes." (Matthew 24:7 KJV, Luke 21:11)

2004 Tsunami in Southeast Asia caused by earthquake in the sea: 300,000 deaths
2008. Earthquake in China
2010. Haiti earthquake
2011. Great East Japan Earthquake: Destruction of Fukushima nuclear power plant in Japan
2018. Pohang Earthquake in Korea
2021. Great earthquake and tsunami in the South Pacific
2022. Another earthquake in Fukushima, Japan

Over the past twenty years, the largest and most numerous earthquakes in human history have occurred around the world.

The Fukushima Daiichi Nuclear Power Plant accident occurred on March 11, 2011, in the Pacific Ocean in the Tohoku region, which caused an earthquake with a magnitude of 7 (a magnitude of 9.0 on the JMA) and a tsunami. Along with the accident at the Chernobyl nuclear power plant, it was considered a major accident, recording the highest level of the International Nuclear Accident Rating (INES), Level 7.

Even now, radioactive materials are continuously leaking from the reactor into the air, and radioactively contaminated water flowing under the reactor continues to leak into the Pacific Ocean. Radioactive contamination in the area near the Fukushima Daiichi Nuclear Power Plant is serious due to the leaked radioactive material.

In 2022, another earthquake with a magnitude of 7 occurred in Fukushima, Japan. As a result, the recovery from the earthquake of eleven years ago was affected.

FIFTH EVIDENCE:

Iniquities

"Iniquity will increase, and the love of many will grow cold." (Matthew 24:7 KJV, Luke 21:11)

Child Abduction: The Kidnapping and Murder Case of Hyung-Ho Lee, in Korea

Lee Hyung-Ho, who lived in a Hyundai apartment in Apgujeong-dong, Gangnam-gu, Seoul, disappeared after being last seen at 5:30 p.m. on January 29, 1991, at the apartment playground.

According to a friend of Hyung-Ho, he saw a man with his back turned on the playground in front of the apartment with him, and when he returned after about ten minutes, neither of them were visible.

And that night, a man made a threatening phone call to Hyung-Ho's father and stepmother, demanding 70 million won if they wanted the child returned.

After making the first threatening phone call, the criminal called the house to see if Hyung-Ho's parents had reported it to the police.

Hyeong-Ho's father, Lee Woo-Sil, had remarried after divorcing Hyung-Ho's biological mother.

He was told to use the car phone and instructed to prepare

money and drive to Gimpo Airport. He put the money in the trunk and parked the car in the domestic parking lot; the kidnapper instructed him to take the airport bus No. 600 and return to his home in Apgujeong, but he did not take the money, using the excuse that someone was in the back seat of the car.

Afterwards, he ordered Woo-Sil to stop the car on Daehangno, enter the bakery across the street, and wait for further instructions. Meanwhile, he called Hyung-Ho's stepmother at home and asked why they called the police.

The stepmother claimed that they didn't call the police, but after the kidnapper's questioning, she admitted to calling them. After that, the criminal did not contact Hyung-Ho's parents for a while.

70 Million Won Demand

The criminal decided that it was dangerous to receive money directly, so he opened a bank account and tried to receive money.

At that time, it was possible to open an account with a fake identity without an ID, so he opened an account in a bank and sent a note to Hyung-Ho's parents with the account number for them to make a deposit.

However, bank employees hesitated when they saw that it was a new account; when the criminal noticed, he fled. Unfortunately, there was no CCTV installed at the bank branch at the time.

The criminal, who failed to receive the money, issued an ultimatum on the night of February 14 of the same year.

The criminal sent a note to Hyung-Ho's father, telling him to put a bundle of money in an iron box near Yanghwa Bridge on the banks of the Han River; the police recommended he mix real money with 100,000 won and a bundle of fake money and put it in the iron box.

However, the detectives confused the location of the box in the process of exchanging radio with each other, and in the meantime, the criminal disappeared with a bundle of money.

The criminal who took the money called and said, "There is a lot of fake money mixed in. He must not want to get his son back. But thank you for not reporting it to the police." He then cut off contact.

On March 13, 1991, a month after the last call from the criminal, the body of a child was found in a drainage ditch in the Jamsil district of Hangang Park.

After the autopsy, the cause of death was found to be asphyxiation. Also, there were traces of assault on the body.

It is highly likely that he was assaulted and killed soon after the abduction.

When it was revealed that the criminal had already killed the child and kept making threatening phone calls asking for money, the people were very outraged.

Child Abduction: The Park Chorong Chorong Bitnari Incident

Child Abduction: Friendship Shenyang Disappearance Case

Sexual Offense: Jo Doo-Soon

Controversy over sexual harassment in the art world in Korea includes the case of a young actress, Jang Ja-Yeon, who committed suicide after being forced to provide sexual favors by her company president in 2009.

The Nth Room Case was conducted from the second half of 2018 to March 2020. Victims in Korea were enticed using messenger apps such as Telegram, Discord, Line, Wicker, Wire, and KakaoTalk. In this digital sexual exploitation case, sexual exploitation was threatened and explicit videos were distributed.

This digital sex crime began in November 2018, when dozens of women were blackmailed and lured to film sexually explicit videos, which were then sold and shared through Telegram.

Of the seventy-four officially known victims, sixteen of them were underage, causing public outrage.

The Nth Room Case and the Doctor's Room Case

The media called this the Nth Room Case, but these digital sex crimes were committed by several individuals.

And the Doctor's Room Incident involved a criminal known as the Doctor, who ran a chat room and charged admission.

Operator God God and Nth Room Incident

In February 2019, a Telegram user with the nickname God God created eight rooms, from Room 1 to Room 8, the so-called Room N.

In each room, sexual exploitation videos were made with three or four female victims; they were distributed through Twitter and other sites; links to Room N were sold for around 50,000 won.

Since then, the captured photos of Telegram Nth Room have been floating around in communities such as DC Inside's domestic baseball gallery, CSAT gallery, and Ilbe Repository.

The Crime Method of *God God* in the Nth Room Case

As long as you have an email, you can create an unlimited Twitter account and use it anonymously. Among the numerous anonymous accounts, there are those who enjoy posting photos and videos that reveal their sexual behavior or parts of the body; they are called deviant users.

God God sends a personal Twitter message with the URL, saying, "Your photos and personal information are being distributed without permission to deviant Twitter users."

In the URL, a fake Twitter login window and personal information input window appear, and when people who fall into this URL enter their Twitter ID, password, and personal information, God God gets the information.

Afterwards, he impersonated the police and said, "You will be investigated on charges of distributing pornography."

However, he asks for a body photo to help him avoid being investigated.

If the account holder hesitates or is not deceived, he uses the personal information and account information obtained earlier to blackmail them and force photos and videos.

The fact that someone will find out who you are in a situation in which you have exposed your body photos using the anonymity of the victims creates fear and inevitably blurs your judgment of the situation.

The videos were circulated in Room N, and films of minors were included.

Group Chat Case (November 2015–June 2016)

Chul-su jung (alias), who was also charged with illegal filming and distribution, is summarized in the table. He was found guilty by the trial court. Here's a breakdown of it in chronological order: However, the date, location, and contents of the filming were not specifically moved to protect the victims.

(Shooting date, filming location, filming content, distribution date and time, distribution target, in order)

November 2015. An entertainment pub in Gangnam, Seoul/ Video of touching a specific part of victim A's body (who consented to the filming but not the distribution)/0:24 a.m. on the same day/ Chul-su jung (alias) (singer)

November 2015. An entertainment pub in Gangnam, Seoul/ Photo of a specific part of victim A's body (who consented to the photo but not the distribution)/0:56 a.m. on the same day/Kim (Club Burning Sun employee)/Chul-su jung (alias) and sentenced to five years in prison)

At 2:15 p.m. on the same day, XXKim, Chul-soo choi (indicted with singer Chul-su jung (alias), sentenced to five years in prison), Kwon (indicted with famous girl group singer's brother/Chul-su jung (alias), sentenced to four years in prison), Park, Heo (indicted together with Chul-su jung (alias), sentenced to two years of probation).

November 2015. An entertainment pub in Gangnam, Seoul/ Photo of a specific part of victim A's body (with consent, but he did not consent to dissemination)/2:15 p.m. on the same day/Kim, Jong-soo choi, ○○kwon, ○○park·○heo group chat room

December 2015. Chul-su jung (alias) house/Victim's back photo, taken without consent/December 1, 2016, 3:35 a.m./Kim

December 2015. Chul-su jung (alias) house/Victim C's photo, taken without consent/December 9, 2015, 2:51 p.m./Kim

December 2015. A hotel in Taiwan/Video of sexual intercourse between Chul-su jung (alias) and victim D (taken without consent)/December 11, 2015, 2:06 a.m./Seung-hyeon Lee (Singer Seungri), Yoo (CEO of Yuri Holdings), kim· Jong-soo choi ·○○kwon·○○Park·○Heo Group chat room

February 2016. Gangnam-gu, Seoul/Video of sexual activity between Chul-soo Jung and victim E (taken without consent)/ February 28, 2016, at 1:07 a.m./Jin soo Lee (alias)

April 2016. Location unknown/Photo of the sleeping victim F, taken without consent/April 21, 2016, 6:35 p.m./Kim○○· Jong-soo choi Kwon○○·Park○○·Heo ○ Group chat room

May 2016. Inside an airplane departing from China/Photo of certain body parts of a crew member sitting on a chair (taken without consent)/May 6, 2016, 2:40 p.m./Group ○○jeong·○○Lee·◇◇kim chat room

The same photo was also shared in the group chat room of Jin-soo lee (alias), ○○Kim, □□Kim, ○○Park, ○Heo at the same time.

May 2016. Chul-soo jung house/Chul-soo jung and Victim G sexual activity video (taken without consent)/May 26, 2016, at 10:20 a.m./Jin-soo Lee·○○Kim·□□Kim·○○Park·○Heo · ▽▽Kim group chat room

June 2016. Chul-soo jung house/Photo of victim H's back (taken without consent)/June 19, 2016, 5:26 p.m./Jin-soo Lee·○○Kim· □□Kim·○○Park·○Heo· Kim Group chat room

June 2016. Hotel in Japan/Photo of victim I undressing (taken without consent)/June 23, 2016, 5:51 a.m./Jin-soo Lee, ○○Kim, □□Kim, Park ○○, ○Heo, Kim group chat room

What do you think after reading it all? The fact of illegal filming and distribution revealed during the investigation and trial process alone shows how routine and serious these crimes were.

From December 2015 to June of the following year, Chul-su jung (alias) went through five different group chat rooms and three private chat rooms to distribute photos or videos he took to a total of fourteen people.

The same person may have been victimized more than once, but you can see that there are at least ten victims, including two foreigners.

The criminal chose places such as his home, an entertainment pub, an airplane, or a hotel in a foreign country. It was filmed and distributed up to three times a day.

Of course, the above contents are limited to the contents prosecuted by the prosecution to the last. There is a possibility that Chul-su jung (alias) filmed and distributed other videos illegally, but when the police started investigating, he had already reset the so-called golden phone.

Chul-su jung (alias) was sentenced to six years in prison in the first trial, including charges of illegal filming and distribution, and gang-raping a woman who was intoxicated with Jong-soo choi (alias).

The court denounced Chul-su jung (alias) and his party for treating the victims as "simple tools of sexual pleasure" and said that their "severely distorted sense of sexuality" was revealed in the Kakao Talk chat room in question.

In particular, the judge pointed out that the pain the victims must have felt when they later found out that their photos and videos had been circulated on KakaoTalk chat rooms was "extreme enough to be difficult to even imagine."

After the sentencing, Chul-su jung (alias) covered her face with both hands and cried for a long time. Whether it was remorse, resentment, or regret, everyone was busy guessing the meaning of the tears shed by this sex offender. She said, "I'm sorry," to the victims at every public trial.

Even in order to keep the weight of those words, he will have to look back more heavily on his daily life, which involved illegal filming and distribution.

(Source: Chae-rin Kim, reporter, KBS News, Korea)

ACT 2

The Evidence by Parallel Theory

Preliminary Questions of Jesus Coming

1. When? What time?
2. How? By spirit or by new name, new Son of Man?
3. Where? Israel's Olive Mount or a new land?
4. Who? Jesus. Have you seen Jesus? Is Jesus white or black or Asian? The Bible says that false Christs deceive many people. How is that possible? Isn't Jesus Christ an inimitable being Who raises the dead and walks on water?
5. What will Jesus do? Raise the dead and walk on water? Identify Jesus through what?

   In the Netflix drama *Messiah*, it is stated they are trying to solve various problems the world is facing. For example, the refugee problem, the US military intervention, and so on.

6. Why is Jesus coming? For what?

   To solve these questions, we think it is most appropriate to compare it with the time when Jesus first came.

Jesus's First Coming

1. When? Were there any signs? It is said that the spirit of Elijah will come upon the preparer.
2. How? It is prophesied that the Spirit of God would come upon him (Isaiah 11), Son of Man = baby (Isaiah 9).

   He is just, and having salvation, humble and riding on a donkey (Zechariah 9:9).

   "I can count all my bones. They look upon me, and they divide my cloak and cast lots for my undergarment" (Psalm 22:16–18).

3. Where? Bethlehem (Mica 5:2).
4. Who?

   Root of David = descendant of David, Messiah = Christ.

5. What? He raises the dead, walks on water, and is crucified for a sinner.
6. Why? God's will, God's love.

Second Coming of Jesus

1. When? Signs are fulfilled.
2. How? The spirit versus the new Son of Man.

   If by spirit form, can people be deceived by a false Jesus?

   Among the prophecies of the Second Coming of Jesus in the New Testament, there is a prediction that it will be like the days of Noah, and there is a prophecy that He will first suffer many things and be rejected from the times.

   How is that possible? How can people not recognize Jesus, Who is the Son of God and all-powerful?

   For that to happen, things must happen that the average person cannot predict.

   For example, Jesus will appear outside of Israel and appear in a form we don't expect.

3. New Where and New Who (Revelation 3:12)

   How did the Jews two thousand years ago fail to accept Jesus as their Savior? There were already numerous prophecies of a Savior in the Old Testament.

Circumstances like when Jesus first came two thousand years ago will play a key role in our understanding of His Second Coming.

As in the case of parallel theory such as Lincoln-Kennedy/Napoleon-Hitler, we come to realize what Jesus will do.

Why? God's love in parallel.

SIXTH EVIDENCE:

False Christs

The First Coming versus Second Coming

> "Many will come in my name, saying, 'I am the
> Christ,' and will deceive many." (Matthew 24:3–5
> KJV, Mark 13:5–6, 22 Luke 21:8)

At the first advent of Jesus, many heretics appeared. Many
heretics cried out that they were the Messiah.

At that time, Jesus and the twelve apostles were viewed as
heretics. People also saw Jesus as a criminal.

In a nutshell, you can think of it as a prisoner serving a sentence
in prison right now.

Parallel to when Jesus first came to earth, many false Christs
also appeared in Korea.

According to a report by the International Religion Research
Institute in 2015, especially in Korea, over the past hundred years,
"Twenty people claim to be God, and at least 50 people claim to be
the Second Coming Jesus."

Representative Korean Adventists

1. Park Tae-sun (Cheonbu-gyo)
2. Lee Man-hee (Shincheonji)
3. Moon Seon-myung (Unification Church)
4. Jeong Myeong-seok (JMS)
5. Ahn Sang-hong (Church of God)
6. Jae-Yeol Yoo (The Temple of the Tabernacle of the Testimony)
7. Hee-Sung Cho (Yeongsaenggyo)
8. Jae-Rok Lee (Manmin Central Church)

Why are there so many false Christs in Korea? Let's look at the main false Christs first.

Kim Seong-do (1882–1944)

Main Point

Kim Seong-do is called the mother of heresy. It is said that in 1923, around the fourth month of the lunar calendar, she experienced the incarnation of Jesus (the coming of God).

It is said that at that time, the root of all sins was in sexual immorality, and it was revealed that the Second Coming Jesus would not come on a cloud, but as a descendant of a woman, that is, the Son of Man.

In April 1944, Kim Seong-do died at the age of sixty-one after being tortured during her imprisonment. She left a will to her family, saying, "God will send another savior to accomplish his will, and this savior will be misunderstood as an obscene group, and will suffer persecution and imprisonment, so visit this church."

Kim Seong-do

Born on July 1 of the lunar calendar in 1882, at the age of seventeen, she married Jeong Hang-jun (forty years old at the time) at 457 Jangjwa-dong, Beo-myeon, Cheolsan-gun, North Pyongan Province.

Jeong Hang-jun was born the third of five brothers and held a post in Cheolsan.

He also had wealth, married twice, and was twenty-seven years older than Kim Seong-do. One daughter was born to the first wife, and two sons were born to the second wife, but due to the pressure of relatives, they were married to Kim Seong-do.

However, after one year, he pretended to eat beef and died.

The first child died at night, and the second daughter was born at dawn the next day.

After that, she gave birth to twin daughters, and on June 25, 1906, the second son, Jeong Seok-cheon, was born.

However, after giving birth to this son, Kim Seong-do began to show some psychotic symptoms. At home, to cure Kim Seong-do's symptoms, he called a shaman and tried various things, such as visiting a hospital, but nothing worked.

After about three months of leaving the church, the psychotic symptoms were completely cured.

Jeong Seok-cheon reports that his mother was thirty-three years old at the time. A year later, when her son Jeong Seok-cheon fell ill and was healed by prayer, this became an opportunity for Kim Seong-do to have a strong faith and formally enter the profession.

However, since her husband Jeong Hang-jun's family is a Confucian family from generation to generation, he was displeased with his wife's Christian faith and severely persecuted her.

According to what Kim Seong-do's grandson heard from his father Jeong Seok-cheon, "Kim Seong-do entered the army on the 2nd day of April in the lunar calendar in 1923 and met the angels of heaven. It is said that Jesus himself died unfairly because of the unbelief of the earthly people, so he was also asked to launch a movement to remove the cross from the church. And ten days later, on April 12 of the lunar calendar, there was a second interview with Jesus, and at this time, he heard that the Second Coming Lord is coming to the Korean Peninsula as a human being in the flesh."

After receiving a revelation saying, "The time is urgent, it will be announced to the world soon," she reported it to the senior pastor.

However, as rumors of this mysterious experience spread to the church and members of the church often came to her, in 1925, she was punished by the denomination and excommunicated.

The root of sin did not come from eating the fruit of the tree of knowledge, but the relationship between men and women was the cause. That is, fornication became the motive for the Fall.

Jesus did not come to carry the cross, but rather to accomplish His will without dying.

God has two major sorrows. The first is the sorrow that He could not intervene and only looked at, knowing the moment when Adam fell, and the second is that Jesus had to accomplish God's will by living and not dying on the cross. Nevertheless, it was sad to see the scene where Jesus was crucified because of human unbelief.

The Second Coming Lord does not come on a cloud, but through a woman's body.

The Second Coming Lord will come to Korea, and all people will come to know Korea as the cradle of faith.

The World Christian Unification Spiritual Association Historic Compilation Committee conveys the important revelation she received from heaven as follows:

1. Liberation of Korea from Japan.
2. The Second Coming Lord will come to Korea, but He will not come on a cloud, but as a human with a bitter body. And that person is Korean.

3. The fruit of the tree of knowledge of good and evil is not a fruit, but the Fall was an act of love.
   In other words, the Fall was caused by the error of love.
4. Men and women should not be inseparable. Because such a marriage is not a true marriage, but a false marriage.
5. The Lord comes to establish a new lineage. Therefore, the mind and body of all who want to receive the Second Coming Lord must be purified. Therefore, there should be no sexual life between husband and wife.

The reason Kim Seong-do came to see that the root of sin was lewdness was that when the pastor of her attending church was arrested over a gender issue, she was shocked and prayed deeply about sin.

(Source: Christian Newspaper, http://www.kidok.com)

1) Park Tae-sun (1917-1990)

Key: Based on Isaiah 41, Park Tae-sun asserts that he is a righteous man in the East, and that the East is not Japan, an island country among the three kingdoms of Korea, China, and Japan, but Korea, the eastern end of the continent, is the place where the Second Advent Jesus will come and that he is the person who replaces the Second Advent Jesus.

Park Tae-sun's mother died when he was nine years old, and his father died two years later, and Park Tae-sun and his brother, who became orphans, attended Deokcheon Church's Sunday School, not far from their hometown.

After liberation, he attended Namdaemun Church and even evangelized the streets as a zealous deacon.

It is said that when he was at a crossroads between life and death due to an airplane bombing at Pyeongtaek Station, he was given the gift of blood cleansing to feel his own blood leaking out in urine and the blood of the Holy Spirit entering his body.

After this, Park Tae-sun's overheated fanaticism and blind faith were out of control, and in 1954, revival rallies began to take place across the country.

At that time, Park Tae-sun, who left Namdaemun Church and became an elder of Changdong Church, held a meeting at the Mu School Association in Seongdong-gu, Seoul, on January 1–7, 1955. He began to criticize the established churches at the meeting.

In June 1955, he refuted Calvin's theory of predestination and left the Presbyterian Church of Jesus, to which he belonged, and organized the Korea Jesuit Revival Association on July 1 of the same year, forming the mother of today's evangelist.

When Park Tae-sun's Jeondo-gwan movement was on the path of derailment, in July 1955, the Korean Christian Federation (NCC) announced that it was a pseudo-religious movement (1956.9.20–25); it also defined Park Tae-sun as a heretic.

On April 30, 1957, Park Tae-sun declared during a sermon that he was endowed with heavenly authority; on May 18, he declared that a symbol of grace appeared in a photograph with a torch; and on June 9, he called himself an olive tree.

On September 1, 1957, he hurried to build a village of faith, saying that in order to avoid judgment and obtain salvation in the last days, he must enter the village of faith. "Because it is the hall of the devil, there is no salvation. There is salvation only in the evangelism hall." On April 6, 1958, it was claimed that Sorae Mountain, the mountain where Jesus will return, was in Sosa.

In 1961, they promised to give each house a car, a piano, and a recorder if they set up a motorcycle factory in Deokso. He established the first village in Deokso, the second village in Sosa, and the third village in Gijang, Gyeongsangnam-do, and accumulated enormous wealth by exploiting the labor and property of the believers.

There are many different nicknames for Principal Park Tae-sun: "Young Mother," "Olive Tree," "Righteous Man of the East," "Overcomer," "Sacred Dew," and "True Savior"; he declared that he is the new God who came to this earth.

In the early days, he claimed to be a "righteous man in the East" (Isaiah 41:2). "The Lord raises up people in the East" refers to Park Tae-sun himself, and the East is the East (Isaiah 41:25). "The place where the sun rises" refers to the Far East of the East, and the Far East is Japan, Korea, and China. There are three countries (Isaiah 41:1): "Islands, be quiet before me," which means the Japanese island nation should be quiet (Isaiah 41:9). "I have called you from the corner of the earth." So Korea, attached to the corner of the Asian continent, is the country of the East.

Isaiah 41:25 says, "I have raised up a man to come from the north." Park Tae-sun interpreted it to mean that his hometown had escaped from the north to the north, and claimed himself as a righteous man in the East.

Also, the name of Park Tae-sun as an olive tree is recorded in Zechariah 4:11–14 and Revelation 11:4, saying, "He bestows the grace of the Holy Spirit like dew on Park Tae-sun, a righteous man and an olive tree in the East" (International Christian News) (1969.9.29).

2) Lee Man-hee (1931-): Shincheonji

Key: Based on the biblical basis, Lee Man-hee claims to be the Comforter and claims to be the Holy Spirit among the Trinity of God.

Lee Man-hee claims to be the Alpha and Omega. He calls himself a missionary who is an apostle, the alpha and omega of Revelation, the Comforter, the Holy Spirit, and a sealing angel.

"The Alpha and Omega refer to the beginning and the end. The beginning is the seed, and the end is the fruit. The beginning is

a prophecy, and the end is the reality. All the secrets hidden in the Bible must be revealed and bear fruit, so that the purpose of God's creation is fulfilled. ... These words tell us that when the missionary of John the Baptist is preparing the way on the Korean Peninsula in Asia, the Holy Spirit of Christ also comes and works there.

"Therefore, we must keep in mind that the person we need to find and meet must meet Jacob (the Counselor: Israel) who is the Apostle John, who is the victor, to receive the revelations of the Father and the Son and to enter eternal life" (Lee Man-hee, *The Reality of Revelation*, Shincheonji Books, pp. 37, 52).

Christology

1) Lee Man-hee claims to be the Second Coming Lord. All of Mr. Lee's doctrines are merely means to make himself the Second Coming Lord. Lee claims that Jesus's coming on clouds means that he will come to some human body as a spirit, claiming the Second Coming of Jesus as a spiritual thing, and that it is the Second Coming that came to him as a spirit, so he became the Second Coming Lord.

"Jesus who came on the cloud (Rev 1:1-8) comes in one flesh (Rev 1:12-20). This person is also born in a spiritual manger just like at the first advent. ... This is how God came on a cloud and came to Jesus. Jesus, who comes like a cloud, comes to a chosen man and harvests wheat (those who keep the word) from the four directions (Matt 13; Rv 14:14-16) to create a new Israel (Acts 1:6-8, Rv 7)" (Lee Man-hee, *Saints and Heaven*, Shincheonji Book Publishing House, pp. 77–78).

Man-hee claims that he is the one who will rule the world with an iron rod.

There are many heretical leaders who deceive believers by teaching that Man-hee is the ruler mentioned in Revelation 12, and he is also the Second Coming Lord, and he is the child who will rule the nations with an iron rod.

"The saying that a woman who has given birth will flee to her own place in the wilderness to escape the face of the serpent and be raised there for 1260 days means that he came first in front of this child, the promised shepherd [note: Mr. Lee Man-hee] from the standpoint of Elijah and John the Baptist" (ibid., p. 221).

Lee Man-hee teaches that those who keep the new covenant and new things will be saved.

Their soteriology is that they must believe in Lee Man-hee as the promised true shepherd and receive the new covenant made with Lee Man-hee's blood. The new covenant that Mr. Lee emphasizes is not the New Testament established by the blood of Jesus Christ in the Bible, that is, the Gospel of salvation, but the new covenant written by the headmaster himself with blood (Lee Man-hee, *The History of Shincheonji Development*, Shincheonji Books, p. 49).

The new work Mr. Lee is talking about is when all churches and pastors are finished, and a shepherd appears and judges him. This is the argument that Mr. Lee must believe in himself as the true shepherd.

"Becoming a blind servant who does not know the new covenant and new things, like a madman, even after hearing only the world's stories and the world's words (John 3:31), they smile and say, 'I believe, Amen,' and then realize, even if the saints who first realized that they entered this holy city and went into the fire of hell, 'Amen, I believe'" (Man-hee, *The History of Shincheonji Development*, p. 107).

"The end of today, the new work and the new covenant of the Second Coming of the Lord are the same as in the days of Adam, Noah, Abraham, Moses, and Jesus at the first coming. And at the Second Coming of the Lord, all prophecies, churches, and pastors will all come to an end. As promised, He chooses one shepherd and judges the truth and lies. This is the harvest time when the wheat is gathered. The shepherds and saints who have not been harvested are those who are judged with tares. Therefore, at the Second Coming of the Lord, Matthew 11:10–15 The last days of religion, where all pastors, churches, and saints will come to an end just like temples."

3) Sun Myung Moon: Head of Unification Church (1920-2012)

Main Point

They call the homily the New Revelation. This is likened to a tree, the Jewish scriptures are the seeds, the Christian Bibles are the trunks, and the homily is the fruit.

As Adam and Eve failed to complete the ideal of creation and fell, the later Adam will come, who is Sun Myung Moon as the Second Coming Lord.

And later Eve is Hak Ja Han, the true mother. It is said that the Unification Church receives life through Sun Myung Moon and Hak Ja Han, and it obtains salvation from physical corruption.

The Unification Church was established in 1954 and originally called the Holy Spirit Association for the Unification of World Christianity.

It was renamed the Family Federation for World Peace and Unification.

The Second Coming Lord, Messiah, and Head of the Unification Church (1920.1.6). Jeongju-gun, Pyeongbuk, was a fanatical student member of the Jesus Church and the Pentecostal Church of the Lee Yongdo School in Bukahyeon-dong, Seoul, and attempted to study the Bible on his own. He also majored in electrical engineering at Waseda University, Japan.

On Easter morning at the age of sixteen, he heard a divine voice and got a divine revelation.

After that, he visited the Israeli monastery of Kim Baek-moon and received instruction for six months (four months, according to Lee Young-heon's book).

After that, Gwanghae Church was established in Pyongyang (1949.2.22). According to God's revelation, the goddess also married Mrs. Kim, despite the best way to live, and the North Korean government officials arrested him for adultery.

After he was released by the ROK Army, he moved south and spread missionary work in the mountains. He recruited Yoo Hyo-won, a theorist who systematized the principles, policies, and organizations of the Unification Church.

After restoration, on May 1, 1954, the Unification Church signboard was hung and full-scale activities were conducted. In 1955, Ewha University professor Kim Young-woon and four other professors and about seventy Ewha students were indicted in connection with the affair with Sun Myung Moon. Five professors were dismissed and fourteen students expelled. On July 4 of the same year, Sun Myung Moon was arrested along with four executives and was arrested for three months; they were acquitted on October 14.

The main doctrine was based on the Bible. The Unification Church has their canon other than the Bible, which is called the homily or the Covenant. It was drafted by Hyo Hyo-won and Kim Young-woon. The Unification Church believes in this as the word of revelation God gave to Sun Myung Moon. However, according to Park Young-kwan, this is a plagiarism of Kim Baek-moon's basic Christian principles.

They call the homily the New Revelation. It is likened to a tree, the Jewish scriptures are the seeds, the Christian Bibles are the trunks, and the homily is the fruit.

There were three eras: the Old Testament Age, the New Testament Age, and the Covenant Age.

Resurrection (Old Testament), Growth (New Testament), Consummation (Covenant, or sermon).

The Old and New Testaments alone are not enough. Based on John 16:12–13, he insisted on the homily as the completed doctrine of the Covenant Age. Its characteristic is said to be the unification of science and religion.

2. Fall

Based on Genesis 3:6, the spiritual Fall is the blood relationship between the angel and Eve. The fall of the flesh is the blood relationship between Eve and Adam.

As Adam and Eve failed to complete the ideal of creation and fell, the later Adam will come, who is Sun Myung Moon as the Second Coming Lord. And later Eve is Hak Ja Han, the true mother. Through Sun Myung Moon and Hak Ja Han, the Unification Church is said to receive life and salvation from physical corruption.

3. Christology

It is said that salvation through the cross is only spiritual salvation, and physical salvation has not been achieved. By doing this, we see Jesus as a failure in the work of redemption and as a disqualification of the second person of the Trinity.

Critique

1 Corinthians 1:18 says the message of the cross is foolishness to those who are perishing, but the power of God to us who are being saved.

In 1 Corinthians 1:22–24, Jews ask for signs and Greeks seek wisdom, but we preach Christ crucified. Christ is the power of God and the wisdom of God.

4. Adventism

The method of the Second Coming after 1918: God was reborn as an infant in Korea.

According to them, the Second Coming Lord is born as a baby in Korea after 1918. Considering that Sun Myung Moon was born in 1920, their intention becomes clear.

In addition to religious activities, the denomination operates businesses in various fields such as ideology, politics, economy, culture, art, academia, media, and education.

In particular, it has a strong influence on the economic sector. Specific details are as follows.

Currently, there are thirteen affiliates listed on the Tongil Group website (tongilgroup.org). They include all kinds of institutional support projects; it is known that there are more than fifty related companies.

The most well-known affiliate of the Tongil Group is Ilhwa, a company famous for its beverage McCall. Ilhwa is engaged in beverages, ginseng processing and export, and pharmaceuticals.

Seongnam Ilhwa, a professional soccer team, is also owned by Tongil Sports of Tongil Group, which hosts the Peace Cup every two years and features world-renowned clubs.

Tongil Group is also actively carrying out tourism and leisure-related businesses. Yongpyong Resort in Pyeongchang-gun, Gangwon-do, Vice Palace in Boryeong, and Chungcheongnam-do are also members of the Tongil Group.

For the media business, Segye Ilbo publishes a daily newspaper, the *Washington Times*, and UPI News.

Other companies belonging to the Tongil Group include Sailo (service management), Asia Ocean (aquatic products distribution), Ilshin Stone (stone development), JC (metal surface treatment agent), and TIC (auto parts production).

4. Jeong Myeong-seok (1945-)

Main Point

According to The Second Coming, "Christians believe and look forward to Jesus coming from the air in the flesh in the clouds, but in reality the Spirit of Elijah returns to John the

Baptist and the Spirit of Moses returns to Jesus. It is not that Jesus, who was said to have come back in the flesh, but selects a central figure from among Christians and cooperates with him as Jesus comes again as the Spirit, so that the mission of the Second Coming Jesus can be fulfilled."

The second division of the Supreme Court (Chief Justice Yang Chang-soo) confirmed the lower court, which sentenced Jung Myung-seok (JMS), president of the International Christian Federation (JMS), to ten years in prison for sexual assault and rape. He was arrested on April 23, 2009.

Jeong Myeong-seok and Christian Gospel Mission are defined as heresy by the major denominations of the Korean church.

It was defined as a heresy in 1991, starting with the Koshin, in 2002, by the merger of the formal arts, in 2008, by the Joint Chiefs of Staff, and by the Methodist Council in 2014.

Compared to the fact that they have been active for a long time, it can be said that the regulation of heresy has been made recently.

Regarding Jeong Myeong-seok, the Presbyterian Church General Assembly explained that "Bible Interpretation, Church, Trinity, Resurrection, and the Second Coming of Christ," and the Presbyterian Church General Assembly were "anti-Christian in all fields including the Bible, Resurrection and Second Coming, and Salvation."

Born in Wolmyeong-dong in 1945, JMS formed a relationship with the Unification Church.

According to the research report of the denominations, Jung Myung-seok was born in 1945 in Seokmak-ri (Wolmyeong-dong), Jinsan-myeon, Geumsan-gun, Chungcheongnam-do, and attended church as a child.

In February 1980, he founded Aecheon Church in Namgajwa-dong, Seoul, calling himself a provider or a teacher, and expanded his activities, mainly targeting young people and college students.

First, in interpreting the Bible, Jung Myung-seok claimed that "established churches misinterpret the Bible, such as interpreting the Bible literally and doctrinal, without considering the times or science."

It claims stories in the Bible are allegorical, saying, "The five loaves are not bread at all, but the word of life, and the fact that the twelve baskets of crumbs remain is that the twelve disciples still have words like crumbs in addition to the words Jesus preached" (The Parables, pp. 11, 14). This arbitrarily distorted the original meaning.

Regarding the church, "Judaism is a spiritual failure, the Holy Spirit has failed in the New Testament era, Christianity is a spiritual failure, and Christianity has no hope (The Parables, p. 145)."

He denounced the church with a bizarre claim that Christianity will bow to him because he was sent by God, showing the typical example of denial, denial, and denunciation of established churches by most heretics.

Anti-Christian heresy across all fields such as the Bible view, church view, and Christology, denies the Trinity, saying "The Father, the Son, and the Holy Ghost are not one in each comfort."

According to the report of the Anti-Corruption Committee of the General Assembly of Presbyterian Churches, regarding the Trinity, in the Intermediate Theory of the Spiritual Realm in 30 Lessons, "The Father, Son, and Holy Ghost are not one in each comfort. If the Trinity is one, does that mean that God entered Mary's womb?"

Also, "The Trinity is the Father (Father), Mother (Holy Spirit), and Son (Son), which is like a human family relationship. Jesus is a man. He is a Trinity, so why did he not know himself? It is because he is a man." In fact, he denied the orthodox Trinity.

Jung Myeong-seok claims that "Christianity has been teaching a false theology that has not solved the Trinity for 2,000 years," but this is a heretical claim that denies the orthodox Trinity belief.

Regarding the resurrection, Jung Myung-seok argues that "resurrection is the second coming of the Spirit in another person's body" in *The Second Coming Resurrection*, which is his claim on the 30th Intermediate Resurrection Theory. Therefore, the body is the body of John, but in reality it is Elijah, and John the Baptist is both John and Elijah.

To him, the resurrection of the body is a resurrection of works, and the resurrection of Jesus is a resurrection of the spirit, which negates the resurrection of the body. Also, "Buddhist reincarnation theory is the result of the resurrection of the Second Coming" and is making a heretical claim that refers to the state of shamanic divine becoming divine rather than the resurrection ideology taught in the Bible.

According to *The Second Coming*, "Christians believe and look forward to Jesus coming from the air in the flesh in the clouds, but in reality the Spirit of Elijah returns to John the Baptist and the Spirit of Moses returns to Jesus. It is not that Jesus, who was said to have come back in the flesh, but selects the central figure of the times among Christians and cooperates with him as Jesus comes again as the Spirit, so that the mission of the Second Coming Jesus is fulfilled."

He also claimed that "Jung Myeong-seok himself was sent to this age" and that "he can roam the spirit world even sitting down."

The report said, "This is an unbiblical claim, and in the end Jesus also denied both the divinity and humanity of Jesus as the second coming of the Spirit of Moses, and Jung Myung-seok himself asserts that he is the Second Coming Lord."

As a conclusion of the study, "The claims of Myeong-seok Jeong of Aecheon Church are anti-Christian heresy in all fields such as the Bible view, church view, Christology, the Trinity theory, resurrection theory, and the second advent theory. You will have to guide them."

5) Ahn Sahng-hong (1918-1985): Church of God

Core: The core doctrine is a mythicization that claims that the headteacher Ahn Sahng-hong is God and the headmistress Gil-Ja Jang is the bride and mother of God.

1. Ahn Sahng-hong, God, and the Second Coming Lord

Ahn Sang-hong was born on January 13, 1918, in Myeongdeok-ri, Gaenam-myeon, Jangsu-gun, Jeollabuk-do, and it is known that he joined the Ansikkyo Church in 1947. As an Adventist, he was active in the periodical group of "setting the date of the Second Coming," a branch of the Adventist church. Ahn Sahng-hong, the so-called God who came in the flesh, died on February 25, 1985, at the age of sixty-seven. Nevertheless, Ahn Sahng-hong's followers spread their doctrine and deceived the saints. According to their claim, Jesus came to David's comfort (Luke 1:32), but He did not complete David's forty-year reign, as He only served three years of public ministry.

Ahn Sahng-hong was baptized at the age of thirty and died at the age of sixty-seven, completing thirty-seven years of ministry, which was insufficient to fill the forty years of David's reign following Jesus.

They also claim that the name Ahn Sahng-hong is God's new name. That name is already recorded in the Bible. The Bible verse they put forward as evidence is, "And I saw a Lamb standing on Mount Zion, and fourteen and forty-four thousand stood with him, and the name of the Lamb and its father were written on his forehead.

"I heard a sound from heaven, like the sound of many waters, and like great thunders, and the sound I heard was like those who played the harp playing on the harp" (Revelation 14:1–2).

6) Yoo Jae-yeol (1949–): Korea Christian School of the Temple of the Tabernacle

Main Point

The headmaster Yoo Jae-yeol put the exact date of the last days. He said that the Second Coming of Jesus will take place 1,260 days after March 1, 1966, when the Tabernacle Temple was established.

Shincheonji Roots Tabernacle Temple, eighteen-year-old leader Yoo Jae-yeol.

The Gwacheon Tabernacle Temple was located in Makgye-ri, Gwacheon-myeon, Siheung-gun, Gyeonggi-do. Later, after the Temple of the Tabernacle was dismantled, the Seoul metropolitan government built Seoul Grand Park there.

Compared to the "Lamb," which refers to Jesus Christ, the head teacher Jae-Yeol Yoo was called the "Little Servant." Seven stars were adorned above the entrance to the chapel of the Tabernacle Temple. These are the seven stars mentioned in the book of Revelation.

At that time, there were seven pastors in the Tabernacle Temple. He claimed that the seven people who entered Cheonggye Mountain with Yoo Jae-yeol, built a tent, prayed, and received a revelation were the "seven angels."

They said, "We are the seven angels who have received a revelation from God," and "We are the seven stars in the hand of Jesus in Revelation 1. It will become the world of the Tabernacle Temple believers." Based on the book of Revelation, the Temple of the Tabernacle also made the last days and eternal life as core doctrines.

Yoo Jae-yeol attracted people by saying, "Now is the last time" and "144,000 people will be saved." He said that when the last days come, the world will become a sea of fire, and in order to survive, one must enter the Tabernacle and Temple of Mt. Cheonggye.

It is said that when the tribulation of the sea of fire passes, 144,000 people will come out of their shelters and form a new world. In fact, in the 1970s, about five thousand people moved into the Temple of the Tabernacle.

At that time, it was a valley in the mountains where even buses did not go, but one or two houses were built, and later it became a very large village.

The house of believers was in the vicinity of the Tabernacle Temple in Maggye-ri, Gwacheon.

In *The Study of Christian Cults* by Tak Myung-hwan (1937–1994), who was an expert in the study of cults and pseudo-religions, the members of the Temple of the Tabernacle "referred to the founder Yoo Jae-yeol as 'God's Comforter, the Holy Spirit of Truth' 'a reaper of eternal life', 'God I believe that he is a messenger who made him a bearer of a seal.'"

The failure of the prophecy of the last days of the Temple of the Tabernacle witnessed by Lee Man-hee.

Man-hee entered Gwacheon Tabernacle Temple at the age of thirty-six. Shincheonji said that it didn't last long, but he had joined other new religious groups before that. (Source: News & Joy).

What is the heretical doctrine of Shincheonji?

What does it mean that there are many false messiahs around the world, especially in Korea?

According to Acts 5:34–39, Gamaliel the Pharisee, a teacher of the law, respected by all the people, got up from the council and commanded the apostles to go out for a little while.

He said, "Men of Israel, be careful what you do to these people."

Before this, Teda got up and propagated himself, and about four hundred people followed him, and when he was killed, all those who followed him were scattered and disappeared.

After that, Judah of Galilee rose up during the registration process and lured the people to follow him, but he also fell, and all those who followed him were scattered.

Now I tell you, do not care about these people and leave them alone, for if this thought and this work are of man, it will fall apart.

If they are of God, you will not be able to overthrow them, lest you become enemies of God.

There are two things to note here. One is that when Jesus came two thousand years ago, He was treated as a heretic, and the other is that there were false Messiahs other than Jesus.

Parallel to two thousand years ago, false messiahs in Korea will annihilate themselves, and if one of them is real, the truth will be revealed.

SEVENTH EVIDENCE:

Cross Again

Lincoln and Kennedy, Napoleon and Hitler lived parallel lives. The basis of the theory is parallelism.

In the Netflix drama *The Messiah*, the person who is suspected of being the Messiah, like Jesus two thousand years ago, raises the dead and walks on water.

Parallels

The process of the first coming of Jesus Christ: Private Life + Public Life, Cross, Resurrection.

The process of the Second Coming of Jesus Christ: cross again, resurrection again.

Is there any biblical basis for this?

Matthew 24:37–44 says, "As it was in the days of Noah, so will the coming of the Son of Man. Before the flood, people were eating and drinking, marrying and giving in marriage, until the day Noah entered the ark, and they did not realize it until the flood came and destroyed them all. There are two men in the field, one will be taken and the other left. You know that if the owner of the house had known at what point the thief was coming, he would have been awake and would not have broken through the house; therefore, you also be prepared."

From these, there will be many people who will not be able to properly meet the Second Coming.

Luke 17:22–26 says, "And he said to his disciples, 'The time is coming when you will want to see the day of the Son of Man, but you will not see it. People will say to you, "Look, there it is!" As it shines brightly and shines down to the other side of the sky, so it will be with the Son of Man in his day. But he must first suffer many things and be rejected by this generation. As it was in the days of Noah, so it will be in the days of the Son of Man.'"

According to the prophecy of the above Bible verse, when Jesus comes again, He will be rejected by this generation just like at the time of His first advent.

Why Cross Again?

Why did Jesus have to come again, and why did He have to take up the cross again?

The reason is human sin. And because He loves us. Because He loves us so much, He gave Himself once more as a ransom.

EIGHTH EVIDENCE:

Resurrection Again

He seeing this before spake of the resurrection of Christ, that his soul was not left in <u>hell</u>, neither his <u>flesh</u> did see corruption.

This Jesus hath God raised up, whereof we all are witnesses. (Act 2:31–32 KJV)

At midday, O king, I saw in the way a <u>light</u> from <u>heaven</u>, above the brightness of the <u>sun</u>, shining round about me and them which journeyed with me.

And when we were all fallen to the <u>earth</u>, I heard a voice speaking unto me, and saying in the Hebrew tongue, Saul, Saul, why persecutes thou me? it is hard for thee to kick against the pricks.

And I said, Who art thou, Lord? And he said, I am Jesus whom thou persecute. (Acts 26:13–15 KJV)

The two-thousand-year history of Christianity is led by the resurrection of the Spirit of Christ.

As I said earlier, He was crucified in parallel and resurrected in parallel.

Like those who witnessed the resurrection of Jesus two thousand years ago, I witnessed the resurrection in the new name of Christ on May 31, 2020.

Just as Saul witnessed the resurrected Jesus on the road to Damascus and realized that He was the Savior and took up the cross for us, so I saw His soul resurrected under a new name and realized that He was the new name of the Savior. And I realized He was crucified again for ten years from 2008 to 2018, in New Jerusalem, not Israel under the new name of Christ (Savior).

ACT 3

Winner Who Endures Tribulation Will Realize New Jerusalem and the New Name of Jesus

NINTH EVIDENCE:
New Jerusalem

New Name of Jesus

Because thou hast kept the word of my patience, I also will keep thee from the hour of temptation, which shall come upon all the world, to try them that dwell upon the earth.

Behold, I come quickly: hold that fast which thou hast, that no man take thy crown.

Him that overcomes will I make a pillar in the temple of my God, and he shall go no more out: and I will write upon him the name of my God, and the name of the city of my God, which is new Jerusalem, which cometh down out of heaven from my God: and I will write upon him my new name. (Revelation 3:10–12 KJV)

As I said before, when He comes back, He will come to a new place contrary to our expectations and thoughts, so many may not realize it.

But He said that the name of the New Jerusalem and the new

name of Christ will be given to those who overcome trials and tribulations (especially war, famine, and pestilence). Giving a new name would mean making them aware of it.

> Which none of the princes of this world knew: for
> had they known it, they would not have crucified
> the Lord of glory. (**1 Corinthians 2: 8**)

I pray that the same thing that happened two thousand years ago will not happen again.

EPILOGUE

I live with four cats (Kamja, Sundori, Maengkongyi, Jeombaki) and my student, Sakai Kim.

I am forty-seven years old. I think to myself every day, Does God really exist? Does the creator of all things really exist? How can we prove it? Why aren't so many people looking for creators? Why are people so uninterested in God's plan?

But I don't know all about other people. And the relationship with God is one to one.

The Americas have existed almost since the birth of the Earth. However, most of mankind began to realize the existence of the Americas several hundred years ago.

Likewise, while we were sleeping, He returned. The Savior has returned. Two thousand years ago, He returned as promised. However, most of the human race has not yet realized it. According to the Creator God's plan, I did not meet Him in person.

We testify of it because we realized His existence and witnessed His cross and His resurrection.

Printed in the United States
by Baker & Taylor Publisher Services